NOW GO
OUT
THERE

NOW GO OUT THERE (*and get curious*)

MARY KARR

HARPER

An Imprint of HarperCollins*Publishers*

A slightly altered version of this speech was given at
Syracuse University's Commencement on May 10, 2015.

HarperCollins books may be purchased for
educational, business, or sales promotional use.
For information, please e-mail the Special Markets
Department at SPsales@harpercollins.com.

FIRST EDITION

Art by Gregg Kulick

Library of Congress Cataloging-in-Publication Data has
been applied for.

ISBN: 978-0-06-244209-3

16 17 18 19 20   ov/rrd   10 9 8 7 6 5 4 3 2 1

For George Saunders,
colleague at Syracuse for two decades,
wise man, wiseass, scrivener, editor,
kind man, bro.

NOW GO OUT THERE

My goal in high school was to stay out of the penitentiary, so if I can go from there to standing up here, y'all can all get yourselves gainful employment of some kind.

Yes, those are your parents clapping.

When I told my pal Doonie I was getting an honorary doctorate, he quipped, "Being a doctor who can't write prescriptions is like being a general in the Salvation Army."

This made me a few notches less terrified about today, which is how poetry works—you start in a scared place and get zip-lined somewhere truer.

The real purpose of poetry, W. H. Auden said, is disenchantment. Not throwing fairy dust in your eyes. It's stripping away what's false so you can see what's true underneath. I like to say poetry has to disturb the comfortable and comfort the disturbed.

So I'll start with a Mother's Day poem for the proud mamas out there. After decades of food prep and tuition payments, I hope you're feeling the magnificence of your kids' accomplishments. And your own.

Let's give it up for mamas. Go, mamas. Magnificent job out there, mamas, and single dads playing mamas—actually and dads, too.

I remember my own son reaching the age of sixteen, and the day he drove away in a car. Honest to God, if I had seen a giraffe drive away in my vehicle, I would've had more confidence that I'd see animal and vehicle come back in one piece.

A BLESSING FROM MY SIXTEEN YEARS' SON

I have this son who assembled inside me
during Hurricane Gloria. In a flash, he appeared,
in a tiny blaze. Outside, pines toppled.

Phone lines snapped and hissed like cobras.
Inside, he was a raw pearl: microscopic, luminous.
Look at the muscled obelisk of him now

pawing through the icebox for more grapes.
Sixteen years and not a bone broken,
not a single stitch. By his age,

I was marked more ways, and small.
He's a slouching six foot two,
with implausible blue eyes, which settle

on the pages of Emerson's "Self Reliance"
with profound belligerence.
A girl with a navel ring

could make his cell phone buzz,
or an Afro'd boy leaning on a mop at Taco Bell—
creatures strange as dragons or eels.

Balanced on a kitchen stool, each gives counsel
arcane as any oracle's. Dante claims school is
harshing my mellow. Rodney longs to date

a tattooed girl, because he wants a woman
willing to do stuff she'll regret.
They've come to lead my son

into his broadening spiral.
Someday soon, the tether
will snap. I birthed my own mom

into oblivion. The night my son smashed
the car fender, then rode home
in the rain-streaked cop cruiser, he asked, *Did you*

and Dad screw up so much?
He'd let me tuck him in,
my grandmother's wedding quilt

from 1912 drawn to his goateed chin. *Don't
blame us*, I said. *You're your own
idiot now*. At which he grinned.

The cop said the girl in the crimped Chevy
took it hard. He'd found my son
awkwardly holding her in the canted headlights,

where he'd draped his own coat
over her shaking shoulders. *My fault*,
he'd confessed right off.

Nice kid, said the cop.

Thank you for loaning us your nice kids.

And kids, thanks for being here. A university is a city of ideas, and we're grateful you became citizens of our city.

Whether your degree is in architecture or exercise physiology, law or journalism or mathematics, by being here you've added something to the conversation that this city runs on the way the body runs on breath.

In the words of great mathematician G. H. Hardy, what you've added differs in degree only and not in kind from the contributions of the great artists and doers and great thinkers and doers across history—from Shakespeare to Toni Morrison, Einstein to Carmelo.

Each of you is a spark that's added something to our little flame and to the world's torch.

And I'm not just talking to the A-makers—the valedictorian and salutatorians.

I'm addressing the squeakers, too, the people who showed up today as if sliding into a base, maybe dragging a few incompletes behind you. Good for you—you made it!

I hope you all learned what you came for and what you didn't. If you're lucky you fell in love here, and if you're really lucky, you had your heart broken, because that made you a deeper person and maybe forced you to find friends to lean on.

Syracuse is now your alma mater—your soul's mother—and we hope coming back here will always feel a little like coming home.

I started out as a squeaker myself. Yet for thirty years I've taught in college classrooms—twenty-five of those here at Syracuse—and the harder you were to work with, the more you taught me and your fellows about the human heart.

Also for thirty years, I've been afraid of not having a PhD. Now the prospect of getting one has turned into the most gut-wrenching weight-loss program in history.

That's how fear works, isn't it? Getting what you want often scares you more than not getting it.

As a young grad student, I worried like hell that I looked like a bimbo; now I'm an old-maid schoolteacher, I worry that I don't.

My point being, almost every time I was super-afraid, it was of the wrong thing.

And stuff that first looked like the worst, most degrading thing that could ever happen almost always led me to something extraordinary and fine.

So on this day of celebration and hope, I want to do the poet's glum-bunny thing of bringing up the deep, soul-destroying fear and suffering that plague every human life, and pass on some tricks I've used to handle such times.

For I am an expert in fear. For the vast majority of my life, I've had an anxiety disorder big as this stadium.

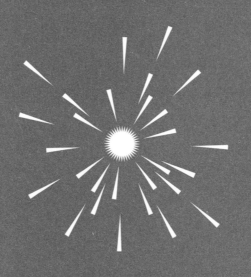

I may look like a calm, educated white woman, but I grew up kind of hard, in a swampy east Texas backwater where the only bookstores sold Day-Glo religious figures and no books in sight but Bibles big as Volkswagens.

Of the six drug-dealing friends I moved to California with in my mid-teens—you can't say we ran away, because when you run away they come looking for you....—of those six friends, four went to the pen, two of those were dead by twenty, another HIV positive and in the Witness Protection Program.

The drugs we all did back then didn't scare me a bit, but should have. They looked like the solution. They were the problem.

What turned me to drugs was partly genetic predisposition—I'm Irish and Native American. But I also grew up in a chaotic household where everybody was opinionated and—because it was Texas—well armed.

My much-loved oil worker daddy had a stroke and lay paralyzed for five years. My mother married seven times. During a psychotic break, she once tried to kill me with a butcher knife then disappeared for months in an asylum. I also ran afoul of pedophiles twice as a girl. Not a childhood people wish for.

But I am not a poor thing or Dickensian orphan. I adored my gambler daddy, who had in his wallet on the day of his stroke my first published poem.

And my beautiful outlaw mother read books the way junkies shoot dope. Plus she got sober at sixty, and showed me how to follow.

In a key family anecdote, the guy redoing my mother's kitchen held up a tile with a perfectly round hole and said to my then seventy-year-old, fluffy-headed mother: *Miz Karr, this looks like a bullet hole!*

And my sister said, *Isn't that where you shot at Daddy?*

And mother didn't miss a beat before saying, *That's where I shot at Larry. Over there's where I shot at your daddy.*

Which is funny as hell

—if it's not your mother.

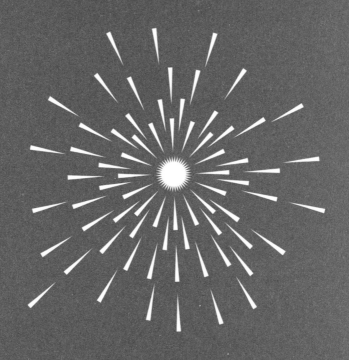

But pretty much every literary project I ever undertook for the past forty years grows directly out of what she and my daddy taught me.

So was being their daughter good for me or bad for me?

I wouldn't have had it any other way.

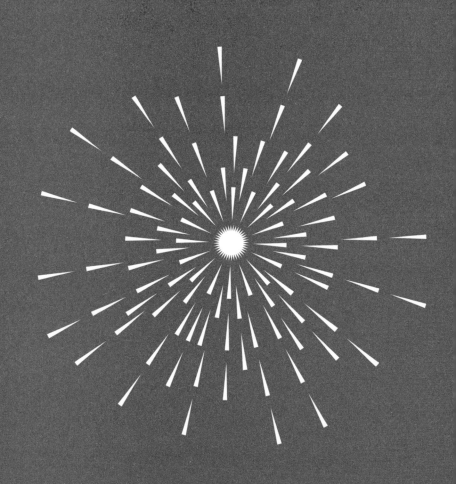

One of the hardest jobs I ever had was trucking crawfish, which I had to do to pay my grad school tuition. Try to imagine the sucking sounds a truckload of forty-pound sacks of crustacean can make. Or the smell of them as I sat on the road trying to keep them alive with wet burlap sacks in 100-degree heat.

If I hadn't wanted to study poetry, I'd never have had to truck crawfish, but poetry has buttered my biscuit.

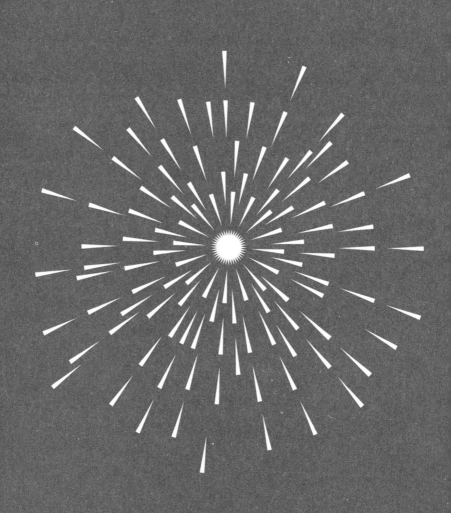

So is it good for me or bad for me?

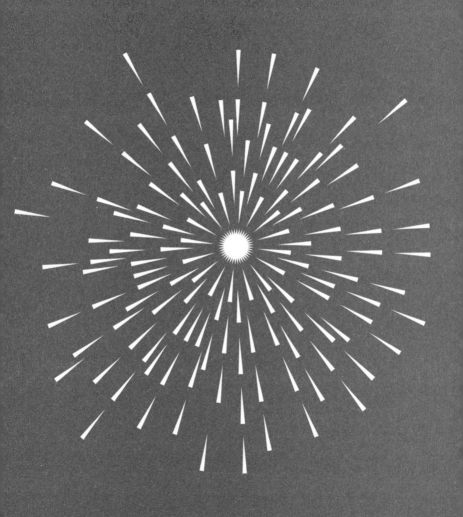

I practically started my academic career at the lowest point in my life. I'd checked into a mental institution for what they called suicidal ideation. While still in custodial care, I got a fellowship to Radcliffe College.

In fact, I had to get a day pass for the first tea, and what scared me that day was that somebody might spy under my sleeve that little plastic wrist bracelet identifying me as a mental patient. Everybody else was sipping sherry and trading ideas, and I spent the whole day sitting in a corner holding my wrist.

That stay in what I call the Mental Marriott wasn't the end of my life but its beginning.

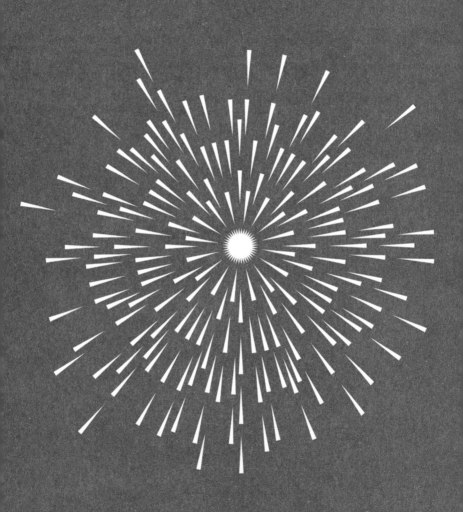

It's where I finally hurt bad enough to ask for help. I started praying in there, and if that didn't change my life, it changed me, and *I* changed my life.

The loony bin is where I learned that as deep as a wound is, that's how deep the healing can be.

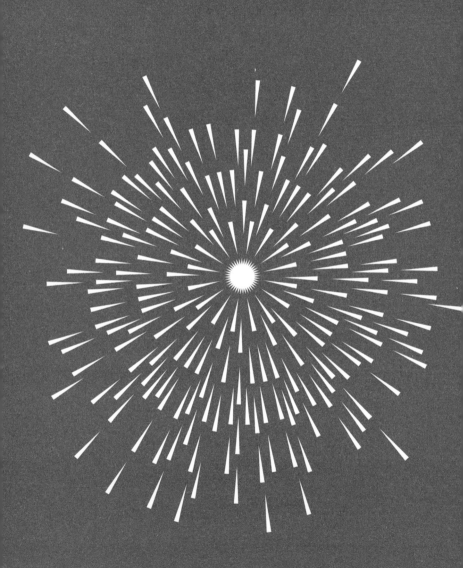

And since this is America, where cash is king, I should say that by telling the story of that journey I made enough to buy a New York apartment and cover my own kid's college tuition.

So was it a nervous breakdown or breakthrough?

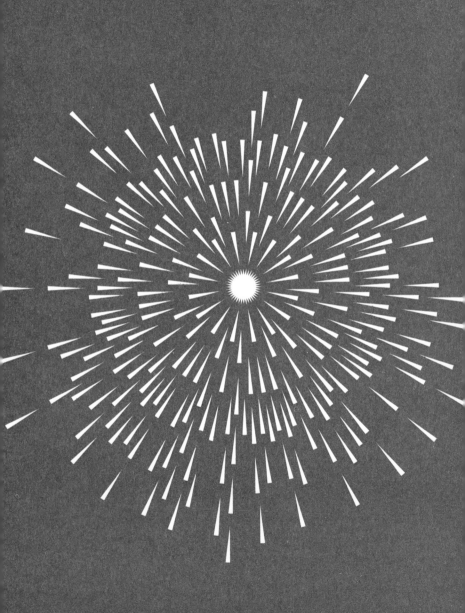

Bad things are gonna happen to you, because they happen to us all. And worrying won't stave the really bad things off.

Look around at each other. It's a good-looking crowd. I'm telling you, y'all look sharp.

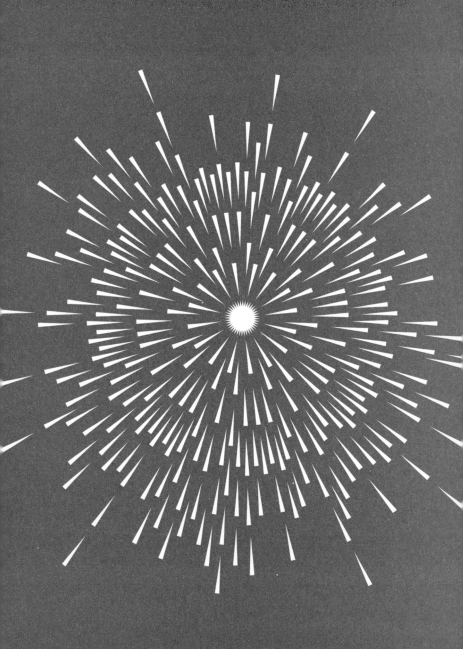

But don't make the mistake of comparing your twisted-up insides to other people's blow-dried outsides.

Even the most privileged person in this stadium suffers the torments of the damned just going about the business of being human.

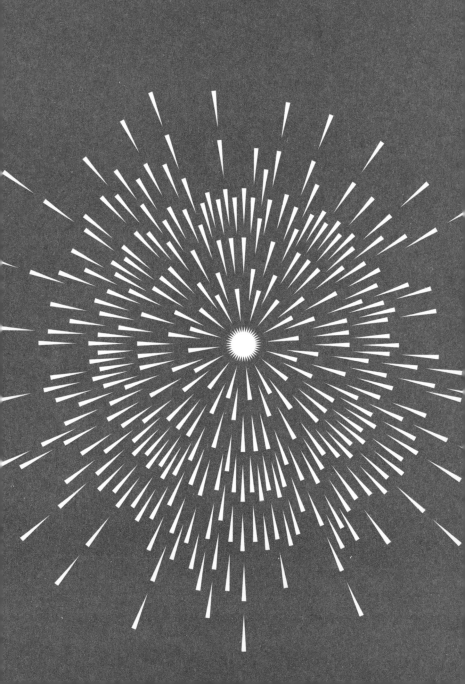

People they adore have dropped dead or suffered agonizing infirmities. In even the best families, loved ones—however inadvertently—fail to show up at the key instant, or they show up serving grief and shame when tenderness is starved for.

Far as I can tell, a dysfunctional family is any family with more than one person in it.

Even at a celebration like this, you might feel simmering inside you some low-level anxiety—fear of not getting the right job or apartment or partner.

Your parents are scared too—that you'll land back on that damn couch!

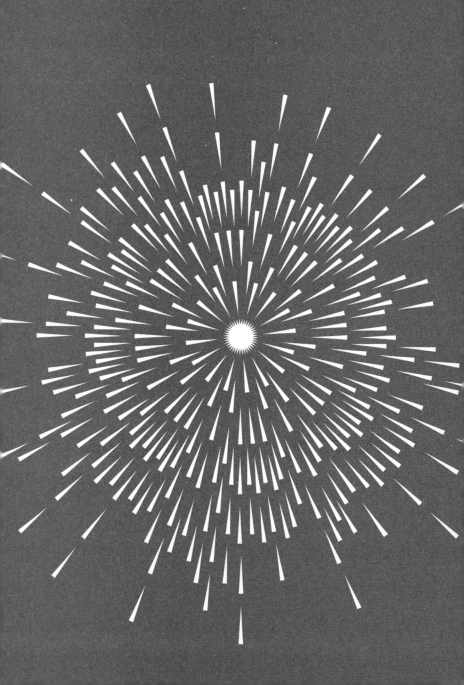

When I was young and troubled, I thought feeling better would only happen when I found enough people to love me. But it turns out finding people to love and do for is way more healing. And that's what my students have given me.

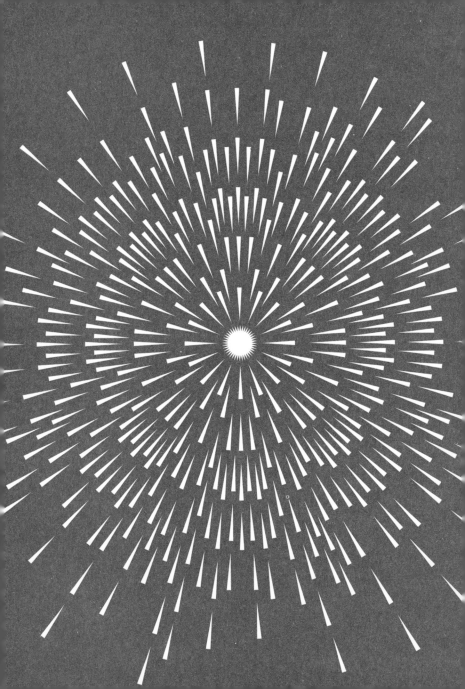

See, the opposite of love isn't hate. It isn't even indifference. It's fear—often fear of the very pain and suffering which we all know are inevitable.

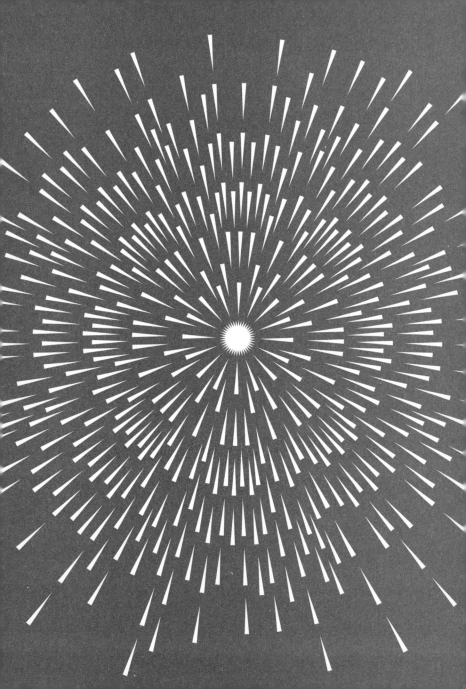

Every major religion tells you the solution to your fear is loving other people, and they're not wrong.

But few religions talk about how truly nerve-wracking other people can be when they're sucking up your subway air or getting your job or stealing your boyfriend. Or just standing in line ahead of you at Starbucks.

That fear and rage you feel for them you'll also turn on yourself.

The same inner voice you use to bash others eventually lands back on you.

Trust me. It'll choke your heart.

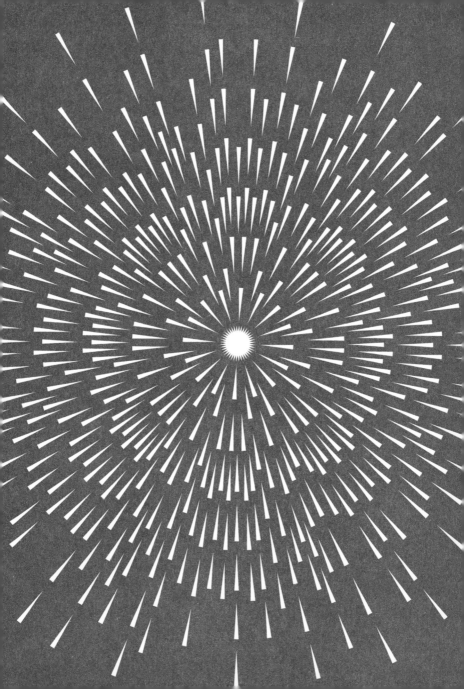

Fear can take that expensively educated brain of yours and reduce it to the state of a dog growling over a bone.

You know the moments. Pulse pounding in your ears, sweat bumping your ribs.

Ask yourself at such times, who's noticing how scared you are? It's this watcher or noticer self that's who I think you *really* are.

That's where your soul is.

That's where God comes in.

That's the place you can draw strength from.

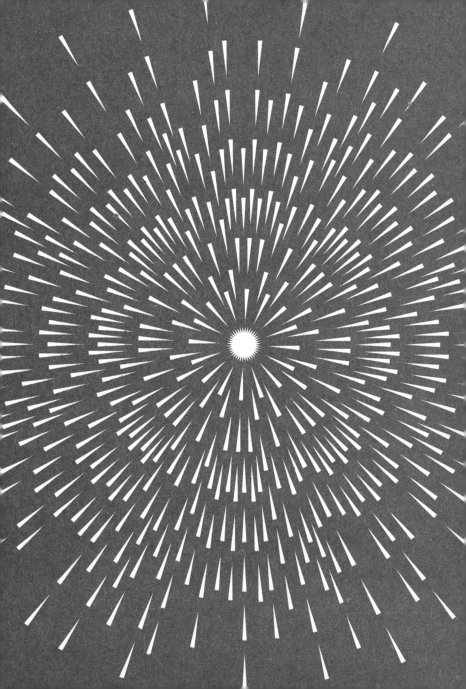

And if I could, I'd like to download in your brains today a hardwired app that would permit you to observe your own fear and rage from inside that noticer place.

I'd like to install a button you could push that could say to you during the bad times, in a really convincing voice:

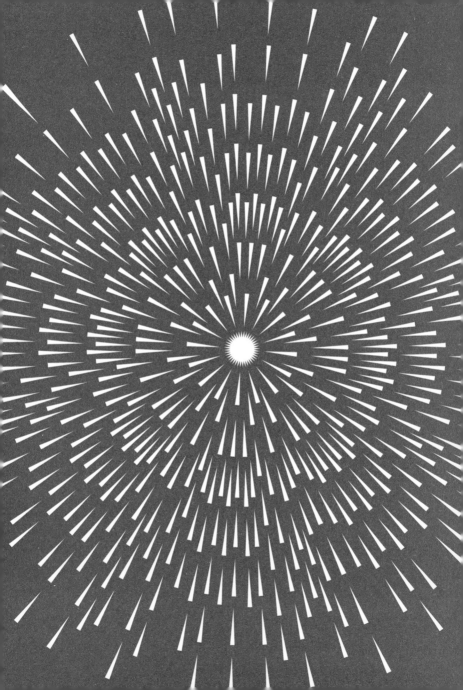

"This hard spell might be the start of something truly great I can't foresee right now because I'm scared shitless."

And if you can get curious about what scares or infuriates you—especially if it's part of yourself— you can grow less scared.

And fast—in the flick of a lash. You can open your eyes onto a completely different world, because you can see it from a less terrified consciousness.

See it clearer, truer.

I'd like to end with a story about the professor who first inspired me to want to teach college.

His name was Walt Mink—yes they named a punk band after him.

I got to know Walt well because in the physiological psych class he taught, I was paired with the most irritating lab partner in history.

Macalester College that year was awash in tie-dye and long hair. This guy only wanted to talk about the neurological superiority of white people over African Americans and Jews.

He had allergies and not the best hygiene. He smelled like a foot. He wiped snot on a lot of stuff I had to pick up.

At one point I went to Walt, who I was sort of shy to talk to because . . . I was an idiot. But I barged into his office hours frustrated and irate and said, "Why don't you just tell him to shut up?"

And Walt said a sentence I'll never forget that has informed my life as a professor. "Because it's my job to put information into his head, and unless I know what's in there already, I can't do my job."

He'd shown me how to replace revulsion with curiosity. How to wonder.

Because of that kid, I wound up in Walt's office a lot.

And because I was depressed out of my gourd, I eventually broke down crying.

And he and his wife helped me to get into therapy and gave me all kinds of easy jobs so I could pay for it—taking care of the department's lab rats or babysitting his high school age kids who didn't need it.

So was that lab partner good for me or bad for me?

Also, Walt took me to lunch all the time, which then seemed like an incredible luxury.

And before I left Minnesota—stupidly dropping out to lope around Europe—I said to him, "How will I ever pay you back for all this?"

And he looked surprised. He said, "It's not that linear. You're not gonna pay me back. You're gonna take somebody else to lunch who needs it."

Now the idea that Walt thought I would ever make enough money to buy somebody else lunch astonished me.

It is truly the greatest vote of confidence I'd ever had. Most people looked at me and saw a screwup.

Walt showed me that a great talent for fear could also mask a talent for empathy.

For caring how others feel.

For tenderness.

There's an unexpected power coming from care
that I choose to interpret as divine.

I hope you remember what Walt said when the world scares you with its barks and bites.

May you leave us more curious about the world and more open-hearted about your fellow citizens than when you showed up.

Being smart and rich are lucky, but being curious and compassionate will save your ass.

Being curious and compassionate can take you out of your ego and edge your soul towards wonder.

Now go out there and buy somebody broker than you lunch.

ABOUT THE AUTHOR

Mary Karr is the author of three award-winning, bestselling memoirs: *The Liars' Club*, which kick-started a memoir revolution and was a finalist for the National Book Critics Circle Award; *Cherry*; and *Lit,* which was a "Top Ten" *New York Times Book Review* pick (and hit virtually every other Best of the Year list) and also a National Book Critics Circle Award finalist. Her book *The Art of Memoir* was also a *New York Times* bestseller. A Guggenheim Fellow in poetry, Karr has won Pushcart Prizes for both verse and essays. Other grants include the Whiting Award and Radcliffe's Bunting Fellowship. She is the Peck Professor of Literature at Syracuse University.